# BEING PATIENT

by Joy Berry • Illustrated by Maggie Smith

*Joy Berry* ★ **Enterprises**

Hello, my name is Roma.

I live with Li.

Sometimes it's hard for Li to be patient and wait for things.

Sometimes it might be hard for you to wait, too.

It might be hard for you to wait for something you want right away.

It might be hard for you to wait
to do something fun.

It might be hard for you to wait to go
someplace special.

It might be hard for you to wait for an important event.

When it's hard for you to wait, you might feel impatient.

When you feel impatient, you might feel restless and cranky.

When you are restless and cranky, you might say or do things you shouldn't say or do.

You might whine, complain, or misbehave.

Whining, complaining, and misbehaving will not make waiting for what you want any easier.

Acting like that will only upset the people around you.

When you have to wait for something, try to be patient.

Being patient means waiting without whining or complaining.

It's easier to be patient when you do certain things.

When you go someplace where you'll have to wait, bring along something fun to do.

Try not to think about what you are waiting for.

Think of something else to do instead.

Be sure to choose something that is okay for you to do.

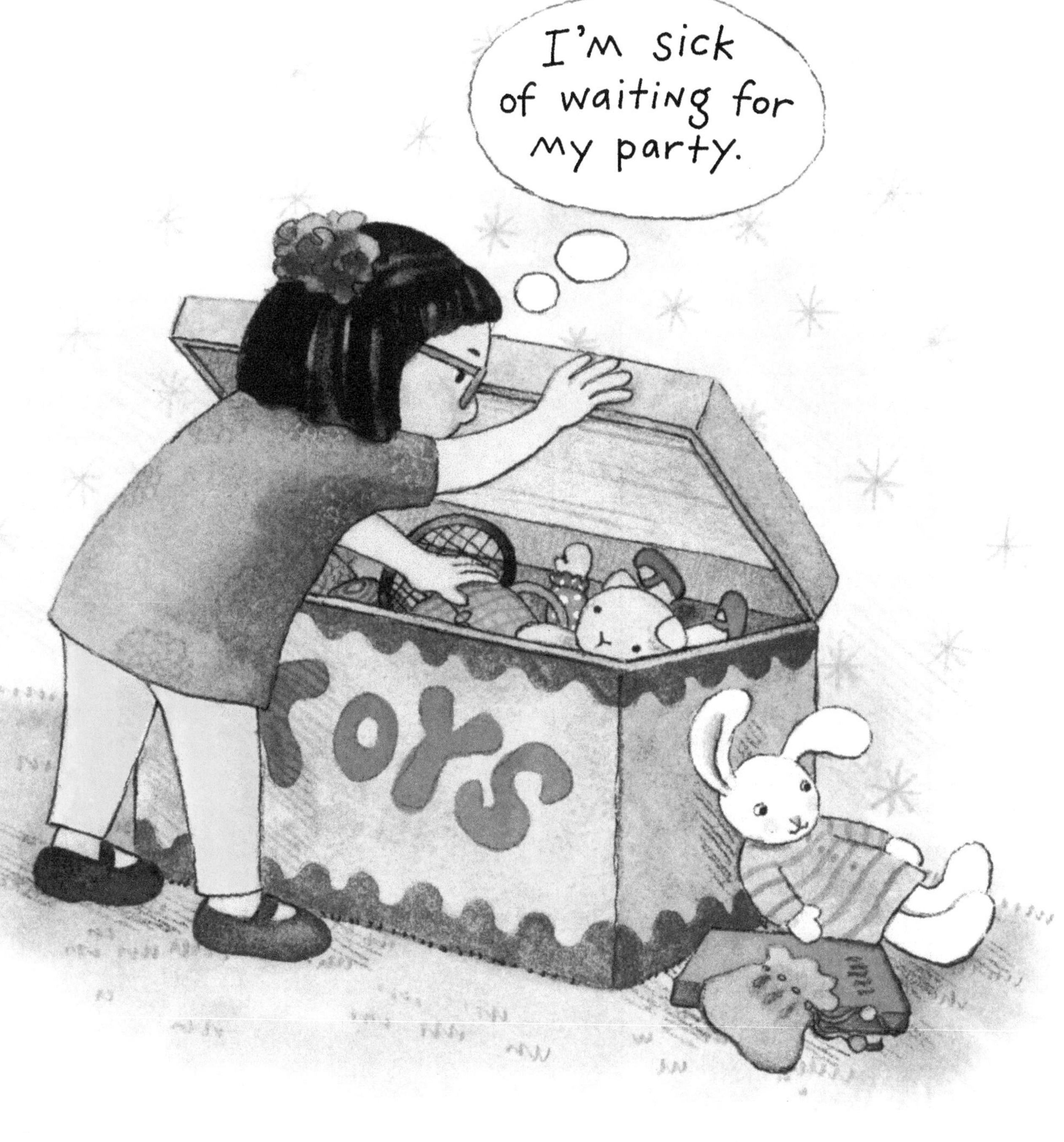
I'm sick of waiting for my party.
TOYS

Time will seem to go by more quickly if you keep yourself busy.

This can make waiting easier.

Sometimes no matter what you do,
it will be hard to wait.

Just remember that everyone has to wait sometimes.

Being patient makes waiting easier for everyone!

# Let's talk about...**Joy Berry!**

**A**s the inventor of self-help books for kids, Joy Berry has written over 250 books that teach children about taking responsibility for themselves and their actions. With sales of over 80 million copies, Joy's books have helped millions of parents and their kids.

Through interesting stories that kids can relate to, Joy Berry's Let's Talk About books explain how to handle even the toughest situations and emotions. Written in a clear, simple style and illustrated with bright, humorous pictures, the Let's Talk About books are fun, informative, and they really work!

CPSIA information can be obtained
at www.ICGtesting.com
Printed in the USA
BVHW011910281122
652963BV00003B/88